A New Life

by
Gloria Copeland

Harrison House
Tulsa, Oklahoma

The Power to Live a New Life

ISBN 1-57794-056-1

KCM-156-1
30-0522

Published by Harrison House, Inc.
P. O. Box 35035
Tulsa, Oklahoma 74153

The Power to Live
a New Life

How can we experience the power of a new life found in our everyday walk with the Lord? The answer can be found in Romans 6:4. *"Therefore we are buried with him by baptism into death: that like as Christ was raised up from the dead by the glory of the Father, even so we also should walk in newness of life."*

I want to draw your attention to the words even so. They mean the same thing as just as. Just as Jesus was raised up from the dead by the glory of the Father, so are we to walk in newness of life by that same glory. That glory is already in us. In spirit, we have already been resurrected to a level high enough to defeat anything the enemy would bring against us. The Father has enabled us as believers to live above the dominion of sin and death.

How has He enabled us? He gave us a new reborn spirit and filled us with His Spirit. *"A new heart also will I give you, and a new spirit will I put within you: and I will take away the stony heart out of your flesh, and I will give you an heart of flesh. And I will put my spirit within you, and cause you to walk in my statutes, and ye shall keep my judgments, and do them"* (Ezekiel 36:26-27). Until we were born again and filled with His Spirit, we were held by the things of this natural world. We were dead to God and alive to sin. Now, we have been crucified with Christ (Galatians 2:20). We have died to sin and have been raised together with Him (Ephesians 2:5-6). The old sinner that we once were has died. We have become a new creation on the inside (2 Corinthians 5:17). And that new creature lives in the image of Jesus Christ, Who is the express image of the Father!

Your spirit man has been resurrected with the same new life with which He made Jesus alive. *"But God! So rich is He in His mercy! Because of and in order to satisfy the great and wonderful and intense love with which He loved us, Even when we were dead (slain) by [our own] shortcomings and trespasses, He made us alive together in fellowship and in union with Christ. He gave us the very life of Christ Himself, the same new life with which He quickened Him..."* (Ephesians 2:4-5, *The Amplified Bible*).

Colossians 2:9-10 in *The Amplified Bible* tells us that we have the potential to become fully spiritually mature. *"For in Him the whole fullness of Deity (the Godhead), continues to dwell in bodily form—giving complete expression of the divine nature. And you are in Him, made full and have come to fullness of life—in Christ you too are filled with the Godhead: Father, Son and Holy Spirit, and reach full spiritual stature. And He is the Head of all rule and authority—of every angelic principality and power."*

God has given us *Himself*, His very own nature, His own substance, His life. We call it eternal life. In order to strike your attention, I want to call it resurrection life. You actually have the same new life God gave Jesus when He raised Him from the dead residing on the inside of you.

So how do we get that resurrection life to affect our daily walk with the Lord and to affect our circumstances? We are to live dead to sin and our relation to it broken, and alive to God in union with Him (Romans 6:11).

"If then you have been raised with Christ (to a new life, thus sharing His resurrection from the dead), aim at and seek the [rich, eternal treasures] that are above, where Christ is, seated at the right hand of God" (Colossians 3:1, *The Amplified Bible*). We must change our affection. If you and I keep our attention on natural things, then the power of our new life in Christ will not be manifested in us. We will remain immature Christians.

We find *how* we are to walk in the power of this new life in Romans 7:5-6.

When we were living in the flesh (mere physical lives) the

sinful passions that were awak-
ened and aroused up by [what]
the Law [makes sin] were
constantly operating in our
natural powers ...so that we bore
fruit for death. But now we are
discharged from the Law and
have terminated all intercourse
with it, having died to what once
restrained and held us captive.
So now we serve not under
[obedience to] the old code of
written regulations, but [under
obedience to the promptings] of
the Spirit in newness [of life]
(The Amplified Bible).

We experience the power of this
new life by obeying the promptings of
the Holy Spirit in our spirits. In order
to serve God in this manner, we must
give Him our full attention.

If you are not manifesting the power
of God in your life, you don't need

more of *God*, He needs more of *you!* If you keep Him shut out of your thoughts, then you will live a mere natural life. God wants your undivided attention so that you will learn to hear His voice. When you hear His voice and obey His promptings, you will be sustained daily by the resurrection life that is in you through the Holy Spirit. He is in you to help you, strengthen you, teach you to mortify the deeds of the body, and lead you into all truth. He is your perfect Counselor.

Many people hear the Word of faith and decide that they will change their circumstances by speaking faith-filled words according to Mark 11:24. What many don't realize is that you can't fill your words with faith. (Union with God through His Word fills your words with faith.) Words become faith

Key

words by hearing the Word of God. Really, by continually hearing and hearing and hearing faith comes, and faith remains. If the world is distracting you from the Father, then most likely your "faith confessions" will be empty words. You are not going to experience resurrection power *unless* you set your affection on Him. The promise of Mark 11:23-24 will still be yours, but it's conditional to your heart condition: *"And shall not doubt in his heart, but shall believe..."*

"Be not deceived; God is not mocked: for whatsoever a man soweth, that shall he also reap. For he that soweth to his flesh shall of the flesh reap corruption; but he that soweth to the Spirit shall of the Spirit reap life everlasting" (Galatians 6:7-8). If you want to reap the quality of life God has prepared for you, you must sow to the Spirit. It's just that simple.

What does the Scripture say? *"...For the letter killeth, but the spirit giveth life"* (2 Corinthians 3:6). If we will concentrate on maintaining our union with the Father, our words will have authority. God's Spirit will make them alive with His power.

Sin, disobedience and living a selfish, carnal life will keep the life from flowing out. Romans 6:14 says that *"sin shall not have dominion over you ...."* You can't keep giving your attention to the things of this world and expect to get dominion over sin. As you set your affection on God and sow to the Spirit, a growing process will take place in you. You will be *"changed from glory to glory as we behold the Lord, even by the Spirit of the Lord"* (2 Corinthians 3:17-18). Then the Holy Spirit does the work in you, and you will begin to look more and more like Jesus. Sin will lose its hold on you. *"This I say then, Walk in the Spirit, and ye shall not fulfill the lust of the flesh"* (Galatians 5:16).

Isaiah 3:10 says, *"Say ye to the righteous, that it shall be well with him: for they shall eat the fruit of their doings."* If you do not live after your new nature of righteousness, then you will not eat the fruit of that righteousness. Verse 11 says *"Woe unto the wicked! It shall be ill with him: for the reward of his hands shall be given him."* This goes right along with Galatians 6:7-8, doesn't it?

Now look at Isaiah 59:1, *"Behold, the Lord's hand is not shortened, that it cannot save; neither his ear heavy, that it cannot hear: But your iniquities have separated between you and your God, and your sins have hid his face from you, that he will not hear."* Sin separates you from the power of God even though you're born again.

Resurrection life will lie dormant in you if you walk in sin.

Until the flesh is brought into obedience by the Spirit, there is war waging in you. The flesh wants to dominate you, and the Spirit is endeavoring to suppress the flesh. But you can win that war! *"This I say then, Walk in the Spirit, and ye shall not fulfill the lust of the flesh"* (Galatians 5:16).

The way to overcome sin and the flesh is not to try and stop sinning. You dominate the flesh by walking after the new life that God put within you. *"For ye are dead, and your life is hid with Christ in God"* (Colossians 3:3). *"Mortify therefore your members which are upon the earth (or, the flesh)"* (verse 5). *"And [you] have put on the new man, which is renewed in knowledge after the image of him that created him"* (verse 10). Walk after that inward man and your outward man will come into subjection to the Spirit. It takes knowledge of God, and knowledge of God comes by spending time in His Word and prayer.

Now, remember that our destination, or goal, is to be like Jesus. Romans tells us that we are predestinated to be confirmed to His image (Romans 8:29). How are we going to get there? Romans 8:1-2 tells us that it's going to be by walking after the quality of life we have received. *"There is therefore now no condemnation to them which are in Christ Jesus, who walk not after the flesh, but after the Spirit. For the law of the Spirit of life in Christ Jesus hath made me free from the law of sin and death."* We have enough of the resurrection life of God to walk in glorious liberty while we are still on earth. We don't have to wait until we get to heaven for freedom from the law of sin and death. The life that is in Christ Jesus MAKES you free from that other law!

"For what the law could not do, in that it was weak through the flesh, God sending his own Son in the likeness of sinful flesh, and for sin, condemned sin in the flesh: That the righteousness of the law might be fulfilled in us, who walk not after the flesh, but after the Spirit" (Romans 8:3-4). The righteousness of the law is fulfilled in us as we walk not after the flesh, but after the Spirit.

"For they that are after the flesh do mind the things of the flesh; but they that are after the Spirit the things of the Spirit. For to be carnally minded is death; but to be spiritually minded is life and peace. Because the carnal mind is enmity against God: for it is not subject to the law of God, neither

indeed can be" (Romans 8:5-7). The Church will never have dominion over death as long as we are carnally minded.

The spiritual mind brings forth life. A spiritual mind marshals itself under the command of God, either by the written Word or by the inward witness of the Holy Spirit. The spiritual mind is open and ready to hear reproofs and corrections from the Spirit of God.

To know and experience the resurrection power of God in our lives, we must constantly conduct ourselves within the sphere of the Spirit. As we do, this constant conduct prompted by the Holy Spirit will make us free from the law of sin and death. If the Spirit of God is directing and controlling us, then there is no condemnation, or judgment, for us. Again, it's conditional.

"But if the Spirit of him that raised up Jesus from the dead dwell in you, he that raised up Christ from the dead shall also quicken [make alive] your mortal bodies by his Spirit that dwelleth in you. Therefore, brethren, we are debtors, not to the flesh, to live after the flesh. For if ye live after the flesh, ye shall die: but if ye, through the Spirit do mortify the deeds of the body, ye shall live" (Romans 8:11-13). The Spirit of God is in us to raise us up from dead works. He will quicken our flesh. If we will give ourselves over to Him, resurrection life will dominate and subdue the flesh.

The Holy Ghost subdues and quickens our mortal flesh. The life of God in us by the Spirit of God permeates outward until the flesh is in subjection to the Spirit.

When Jesus was crucified, our old man was crucified. The Spirit of God

15

is in us to enforce the death of our old man. But the Holy Spirit will not subdue our flesh on His own. He helps us when we consider ourselves dead to sin and alive to God. He is in us to teach and train us how to live habitually after this divine life that we have been given.

It starts with our everyday life. We must allow the Holy Spirit to lead us in the everyday affairs of life and lead us into mortifying the deeds of the body.

If you don't know how to be led by the Spirit, make a decision to learn. Draw near to Him, and He will draw near to you. He will teach you. Tell the Lord, "I want to hear Your voice. I want to do what You tell me to do. I want to walk in Your resurrection power. I desire to experience the power to live a new life every day. By a decision of my heart, I put down the dictates of my flesh and mortify the deeds of the body. By the power of God, I receive a Holy Ghost refreshing in my life. In Jesus' Name!"

Then put into your life things that you know are the will of God: time in prayer and in the Word. Then be quick to hear and adhere to the written Word and the promptings of the Spirit within you.

Prayer for Salvation and Baptism in the Holy Spirit

Heavenly Father, I come to You in the Name of Jesus. Your Word says, *"Whosoever shall call on the name of the Lord shall be saved"* (Acts 2:21). I am calling on You. I pray and ask Jesus to come into my heart and be Lord over my life, according to Romans 10:9-10—*"If thou shalt confess with thy mouth the Lord Jesus, and shalt believe in thine heart that God hath raised him from the dead, thou shalt be saved. For with the heart man believeth unto righteousness; and with the mouth confession is made unto salvation."* I do that now. I confess that Jesus is Lord, and I believe in my heart that God raised Him from the dead.

I am now reborn! I am a Christian—a child of Almighty God! I am saved! You also said in Your Word, *"If ye then, being evil, know how to give good gifts unto your children: HOW MUCH MORE shall your heavenly Father give the Holy Spirit to them that ask him?"* (Luke 11:13). I'm also asking You to fill me with the Holy Spirit. Holy Spirit, rise up within me as I praise God. I fully expect to speak with other tongues as You give me utterance (Acts 2:4).

Begin to praise God for filling you with the Holy Spirit. Speak those words and syllables you receive—not in your own language, but the language given to you by the Holy Spirit. You have to use your own voice. God will not force you to speak. Worship and praise Him in your heavenly language—in other tongues.

Continue with the blessing God has given you and pray in tongues each day.

You are a born-again, Spirit-filled believer. You'll never be the same!

Find a good Word of God preaching church, and become a part of a church family who will love and care for you as you love and care for them.

We need to be connected to each other. It increases our strength in God. It's God's plan for us.

About the Author

Gloria Copeland is a noted author and minister of the gospel whose teaching ministry is known throughout the world. Believers worldwide know her through Believer's Conventions, Victory Campaigns, magazine articles, teaching tapes and videos, and the daily and Sunday believers Voice of Victory television broadcast, which she hosts with her husband Kenneth Copeland. She is known for "Healing School," which she began teaching and hosting in 1979 at KCM Meetings. Gloria delivers the Word of God and the keys to victorious Christian living to millions of people every year.

Gloria has written many books, including God's Will for You, Hidden Treasures, God's Will is Prosperity, Walk in the Spirit and Living Contact. She has also co-authored several books with her husband including Family Promises, Healing Promises, and the best selling daily devotional Pursuit of His Presence.

She holds an honorary Doctorate from Oral Roberts University. In 1994, Gloria was voted Christian Woman of the year, an honor conferred on women whose example demonstrated outstanding Christian leadership. Gloria is also co-founder and vice-president of Kenneth Copeland Ministries in Fort Worth, Texas.

Learn more about Kenneth Copeland Ministries by visiting our website at:
www.kcm.org

Books Available from Kenneth Copeland Ministries

by Kenneth Copeland
* A Ceremony of Marriage
  A Matter of Choice
  Covenant of Blood
  Faith and Patience—The Power Twins
* Freedom From Fear
  Giving and Receiving
  Honor—Walking in Honesty, Truth and Integrity
  How to Conquer Strife
  How to Discipline Your Flesh
  How to Receive Communion
  Living at the End of Time—A Time of Supernatural Increase
  Love Never Fails
  Managing God's Mutual Funds
* Now Are We in Christ Jesus
* Our Covenant With God
  Partnership, Sharing the Vision—Sharing the Grace
* Prayer—Your Foundation for Success
* Prosperity: The Choice Is Yours
  Rumors of War
* Sensitivity of Heart
* Six Steps to Excellence in Ministry
* Sorrow Not! Winning Over Grief and Sorrow
* The Decision Is Yours
* The Force of Faith
  The Force of Righteousness
  The Image of God in You
  The Laws of Prosperity
* The Mercy of God
  The Miraculous Realm of God's Love
  The Outpouring of the Spirit—The Result of Prayer
* The Power of the Tongue
  The Power to Be Forever Free
  The Troublemaker
* The Winning Attitude
  Turn Your Hurts Into Harvests
* Welcome to the Family
* You Are Healed!
  Your Right-Standing With God

by Gloria Copeland
* And Jesus Healed Them All
  Are You Listening?
  Be A Vessel of Honor
  Are You Ready?
  Build Your Financial Foundation
  Fight On!
  Go With the Flow
  God's Prescription for Divine Health
  God's Success Formula
  God's Will for You
  God's Will for Your Healing
  God's Will Is Prosperity
* God's Will Is the Holy Spirit
  Grace That Makes Us Holy
* Harvest of Health
  Hearing From Heaven
  Hidden Treasures
  Living Contact
  Living in Heaven's Blessings Now
* Love—The Secret to Your Success
  No Deposit—No Return

Pleasing the Father
Pressing In—It's Worth It All
Shine On!
The Power to Live a New Life
The Unbeatable Spirit of Faith
* Walk in the Spirit
Walk With God
Well Worth the Wait
Your Promise of Protection

Books Co-Authored by Kenneth and Gloria Copeland
Family Promises
Healing Promises
Prosperity Promises
Protection Promises

* From Faith to Faith—A Daily Guide to Victory
From Faith to Faith—A Perpetual Calendar

One Word From God Series
• One Word From God Can Change Your Destiny
• One Word From God Can Change Your Family
• One Word From God Can Change Your Finances
• One Word From God Can Change Your Formula for Success
• One Word From God Can Change Your Health
• One Word From God Can Change Your Nation
• One Word From God Can Change Your Prayer Life
• One Word From God Can Change Your Relationships

Load Up Devotional

Over The Edge—A Youth Devotional
Over the Edge Xtreme Planner for Students—
    Designed for the School Year

Pursuit of His Presence—A Daily Devotional
Pursuit of His Presence—A Perpetual Calendar

Other Books Published by KCP
The First 30 Years—A Journey of Faith
    The story of the lives of Kenneth and Gloria Copeland.
Real People. Real Needs. Real Victories.
    A book of testimonies to encourage your faith.

John G. Lake—His Life, His Sermons, His Boldness of Faith
The Holiest of All by Andrew Murray
The New Testament in Modern Speech by Richard Francis Weymouth

Products Designed for Today's Children and Youth
Baby Praise Board Book
Baby Praise Christmas Board Book
Noah's Ark Coloring Book
The Best of *Shout!* Adventure Comics
The *Shout!* Joke Book
The *Shout!* Super-Activity Book

***Commander Kellie and the Superkids*ₛₘ Books:**
The SWORD Adventure Book
*Commander Kellie and the Superkids*ₛₘ Series
    Middle Grade Novels by Christopher P.N. Maselli

    #1 The Mysterious Presence
    #2 The Quest for the Second Half
    #3 Escape From Jungle Island
    #4 In Pursuit of the Enemy
    #5 Caged Rivalry
    #6 Mystery of the Missing Junk

*Available in Spanish

World Offices
of Kenneth Copeland Ministries

For more information and a free catalog,
please write the office nearest you.

Kenneth Copeland Ministries
Fort Worth, Texas 76192-0001

Kenneth Copeland
Locked Bag 2600
Mansfield Delivery Centre
QUEENSLAND 4122
AUSTRALIA

Kenneth Copeland
Post Office Box 15
BATH
BA1 1GD
ENGLAND U.K.

Kenneth Copeland
Private Bag X 909
FONTAINEBLEAU 2032
REPUBLIC OF SOUTH AFRICA

Kenneth Copeland
Post Office Box 378
SURREY, BC V3T 5B6
CANADA

UKRAINE
L'VIV 290000
Post Office Box 84
Kenneth Copeland
L'VIV 290000
UKRAINE

The Harrison House Vision

Proclaiming the truth and the power
Of the Gospel of Jesus Christ
With excellence;

Challenging Christians to
Live victoriously,
Grow spiritually,
Know God intimately.